W9-AOX-773

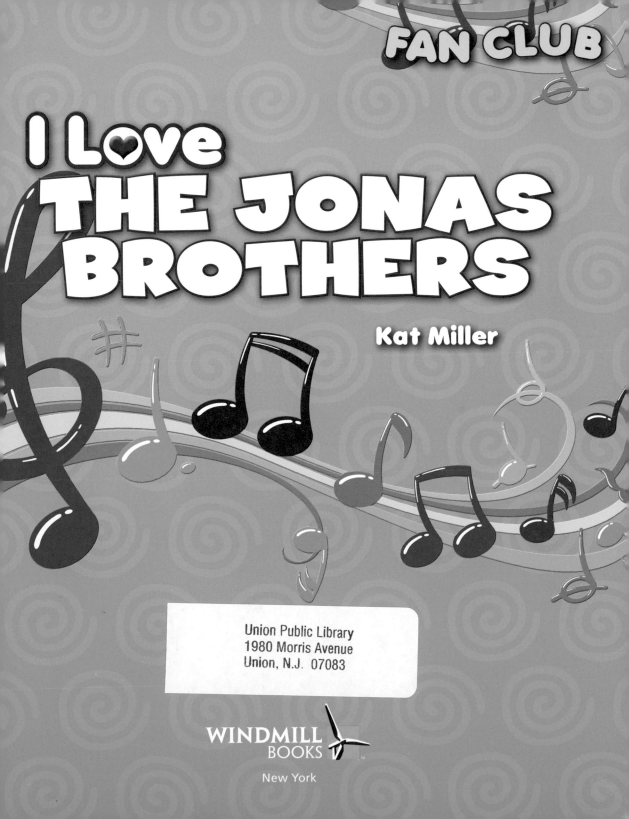

FAN CLUB

I ❤ove
THE JONAS
BROTHERS

Kat Miller

WINDMILL BOOKS

New York

Published in 2011 by Windmill Books, LLC
303 Park Avenue South, Suite # 1280, New York, NY 10010-3657

CREDITS:
Editor: Jennifer Way
Book Design: Erica Clendening and Greg Tucker
Photo Research: Ashley Burrell

Photo Credits: Cover, pp. 10–11, 12, 20–21, 22 Rob Hoffman/JBE/Getty Images; p. 4 Kevin Mazur/TCA 2009/WireImage/Getty Images; pp. 5, 6, 9, 13, 15, 16, 19 (top) Shutterstock.com; pp. 6–7 Frank Micelotta/Getty Images; p. 8 Jeffrey Mayer/WireImage/Getty Images; p. 14 Steve Granitz/WireImage/Getty Images; p. 17 Mike Marsland/WireImage/Getty Images; p. 18 Peter Larsen/WireImage/ Getty Images; p. 19 (bottom) Paul Morigi/WireImages/Getty Images.

Library of Congress Cataloging-in-Publication Data

Miller, Kat.
  I love the Jonas Brothers / by Kat Miller.
       p. cm. — (Fan club)
  Includes index.
  ISBN 978-1-61533-048-5 (library binding) — ISBN 978-1-61533-049-2 (pbk.) — ISBN 978-1-61533-050-8 (6-pack)
  1. Jonas Brothers—Juvenile literature. 2. Rock musicians—United States—Biography—Juvenile literature. I. Title.
  ML3930.J62M55 2011
  782.42164092'2—dc22

[B]

9/11   c

                    2010006169

Manufactured in the United States of America

For more great fiction and nonfiction, go to windmillbooks.com.

CPSIA Compliance Information: Batch #S10W: For further information contact Windmill Books, New York, New York at 1-866-478-0556.

Contents

A Band of Brothers

Have you ever dreamed about being in a band? Pop stars get to meet other **celebrities** and play shows for happy fans. Being a star is hard work, though. You need people around whom you trust. The Jonas Brothers are lucky. Not only are they huge stars, they are always there for each other.

Kevin

Joe

Nick

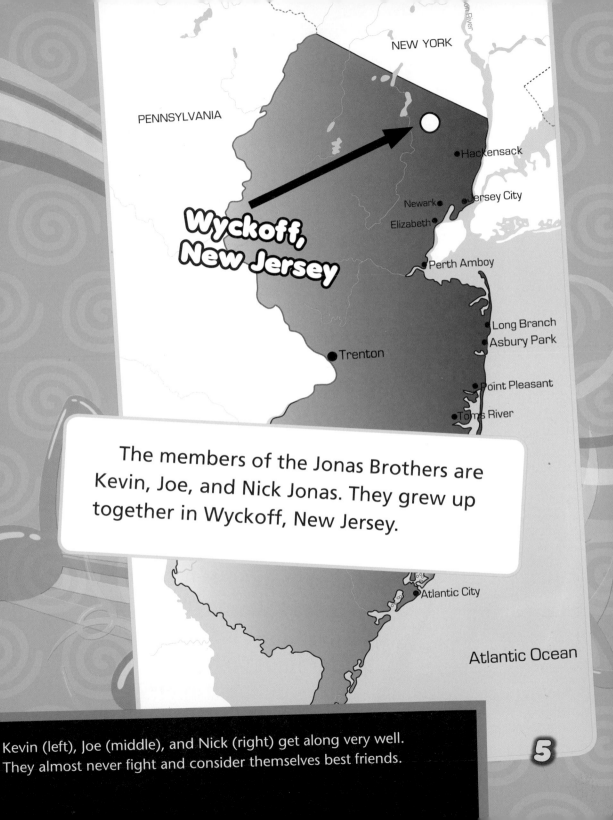

NEW YORK

PENNSYLVANIA

Wyckoff, New Jersey

Hackensack

Newark
Elizabeth
Jersey City

Perth Amboy

Long Branch
Asbury Park

Trenton

Point Pleasant

Toms River

The members of the Jonas Brothers are Kevin, Joe, and Nick Jonas. They grew up together in Wyckoff, New Jersey.

Atlantic City

Atlantic Ocean

Kevin (left), Joe (middle), and Nick (right) get along very well.
They almost never fight and consider themselves best friends.

Kevin Jonas

The oldest of the Jonas brothers is Kevin Jonas. His full name is Paul Kevin Jonas II. He was named after his father. Kevin was born on November 5, 1987.

Les Paul

Kevin is the lead guitarist for the Jonas Brothers. Sometimes he sings **backup**, too. Kevin started playing the guitar when he was twelve. He learned to play the guitar pretty much on his own. Today, Kevin collects guitars. His favorite type of guitar is Gibson's Les Paul guitar.

6

Kevin Jonas, seen here, loves playing the guitar.
Over the years, he has worked hard to become
a better guitar player.

7

Joe Jonas

Lots of people say that Joe is the best-looking of the Jonas brothers. He was born on August 15, 1989, in Casa Grande, Arizona. He is one of the band's lead singers. He is known for his lively singing. He sometimes dances onstage, too.

Joe likes clowning around and being funny. In fact, he thought about becoming a **comedian** when he was younger. He also likes working out, jogging, and making movies.

Left: Joe, seen here, likes many kinds of music. Like many people in bands, he is also interested in cool clothes. Above: Joe was born in Casa Grande, Arizona. The city is known for its beautiful desert scenery.

Nick Jonas

Nick Jonas is the Jonas Brothers' other lead singer. Nick was born on September 16, 1992. His full name is Nicholas Jerry Jonas. Though he is the youngest band member, Nick has played music the longest.

As a kid, Nick **performed** in Broadway **musicals**. In 2002, he recorded a Christmas

Nick Jonas, seen here, is the main songwriter for the Jonas Brothers. He loves music and knows a lot about it.

song. Soon after, a record company **signed** him. When they heard Nick sing with his brothers, they suggested that they form a band. The Jonas Brothers was born!

Rising Stars

In 2006, the Jonas Brothers put out their first **album**. It was called *It's About Time*. It included the song "Mandy," which had already become a hit for them.

The next year, the band came out with their second album, *Jonas Brothers*. Around the time the album came out, the brothers were guest stars on the TV show *Hannah Montana*. This helped new people learn about them. Soon after, they **toured** with the show's star, Miley Cyrus.

The Jonas Brothers performed with Miley Cyrus on her Best of Both Worlds Tour. Here, Nick is singing with Miley.

The Jonas Brothers came out with their third album, *A Little Bit Longer*, in 2008. Their fans loved it! When the album first came out, it was the best-selling album in the country. Next, the brothers went on tour. By this point, they were playing for millions of screaming fans.

In 2009, the band put out *Lines, Vines and Trying Times*. They explored new kinds of music on the album. It was another big hit.

After their third album came out, the Jonas Brothers became superstars. Here they are at the 2008 Teen Choice Awards. They won six awards there!

The Jonas Brothers live in Los Angeles, California. Their TV show *JONAS*, is filmed in Los Angeles.

Though they are best-known as singers, Kevin, Joe, and Nick are all also actors. In 2008, they were all in a TV movie called *Camp Rock*. Joe starred as a rock star named Shane Gray. His brothers played members of Shane's band. *Camp Rock* was a huge hit with kids.

By 2009, the brothers were so well-known that they got their own TV show. On *JONAS*, they play the Lucas brothers, who are in a band together.

Here are the Jonas Brothers at the London, United Kingdom, premiere of *Camp Rock*.

Giving Back

Their music has made the Jonas brothers rich and famous. They want to use their fame and money to help others. To do so, they formed the Change for the Children Foundation. Through this group, each brother works for a cause.

Kevin tries to get people to **volunteer**. Joe supports the Special Olympics. This is a sports event for people with special needs. Nick teaches kids who have **diabetes**, as he does, to care for themselves right.

Joe Jonas is meeting with a Special Olympian and a Special Olympics volunteer.

19

Busy Brothers

Though they are still close, Kevin, Joe, and Nick now do more things on their own. Nick formed the band Nick Jonas and the Administration. Joe was a guest judge on the show *American Idol*. In December 2009, Kevin married Danielle Deleasa.

Here are the Jonas Brothers performing together in November 2009. They not only play songs together, they often write songs together, too.

The brothers still love singing together, though. They still act together, too. In 2010 they all appeared in *Camp Rock 2: The Final Jam* and season two of *JONAS*. They know their fans will always cheer them on!

Just Like Me!

1 Thanksgiving is Nick's favorite holiday, while Kevin's is Christmas.

2 Kevin, Joe, and Nick all like listening to music. Nick's favorite singer is Stevie Wonder. Joe likes Johnny Lang and Switchfoot. John Mayer is Kevin's favorite singer.

3 Joe Jonas's favorite candies are Tootsie Rolls. Kevin likes Butterfingers. Gummi worms are Nick's favorites.

4 Nick likes baseball and tennis. Joe's favorite sport is soccer. Kevin likes badminton.

5 Kevin's favorite food is sushi. Nick likes steak best. Crepes are Joe's favorite food.

Glossary

album (AL-bum) A recording or group of songs.

backup (BAK-uhp) In the background.

celebrities (seh-LEH-breh-teez) Famous people.

comedian (kuh-MEE-dee-un) A person whose job is to be funny.

diabetes (dy-uh-BEE-teez) A sickness in which a person's body cannot take in sugar and starch normally.

musicals (MYOO-zih-kulz) Plays or movies that tell a story with music.

performed (per-FORMD) Did something for other people to watch.

signed (SYND) To have been given a record deal.

toured (TORD) Played shows in many different towns.

volunteer (vah-lun-TEER) To give one's time without pay.

Index

Read More

Johns, Michael-Anne. *Just Jonas! The Jonas Brothers Up Close and Personal*. New York: Scholastic, Inc., 2008.

Keedle, Jayne. *Jonas Brothers*. Today's Superstars. Strongsville, OH: Gareth Stevens Publishing, 2009.

Mattern, Joanne. *The Jonas Brothers*. Hockessin, DE. Mitchell Lane Publishers, Inc., 2008.

Rawson, Katherine. *The Jonas Brothers*. Kid Stars! New York: PowerKids Press, 2009.

Web Sites

For Web resources related to the subject of this book, go to: www.windmillbooks.com/weblinks and select this book's title.